May your creativity flow with the force of a mighty river, may your dreams shine as brightly as the stars and may your laughter reverberate, painting the world with unbridled joy. As you dip your brushes into the palette of possibilities, remember that, like the mighty lions depicted within, your artistic spirit exudes strength and courage. Each brushstroke brings the power and majesty of these magnificent creatures to the canvas of wonder, celebrating the indomitable strength that resides within.

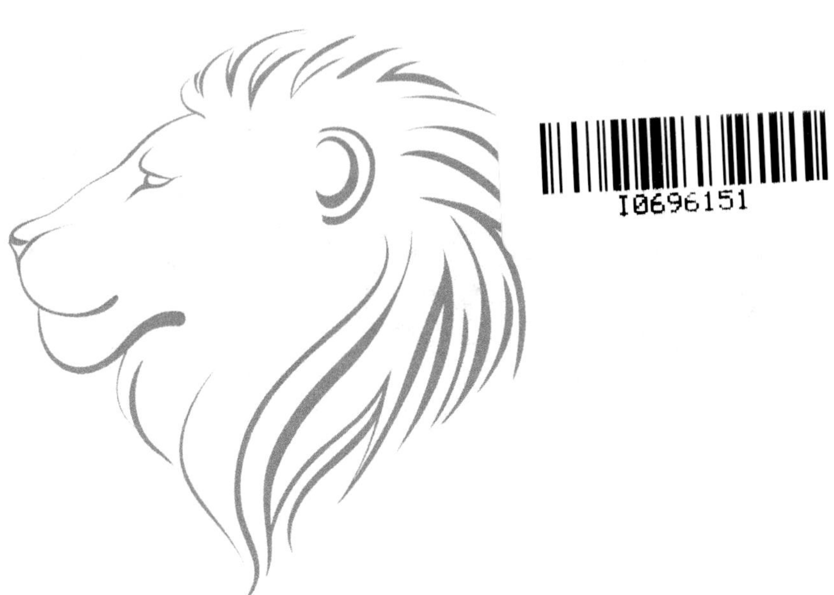

italo_Henrique

2024

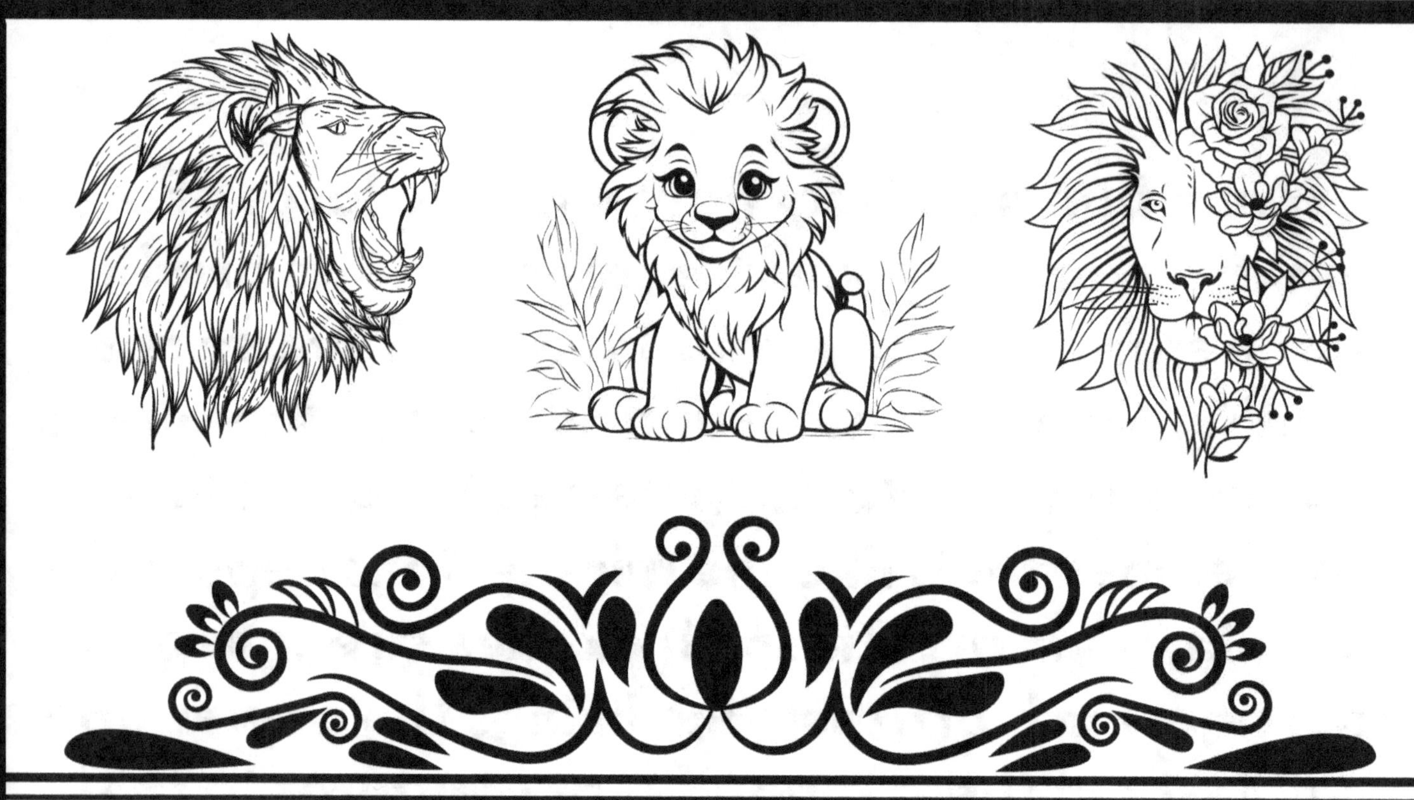

THIS BOOK BELONGS TO:

____

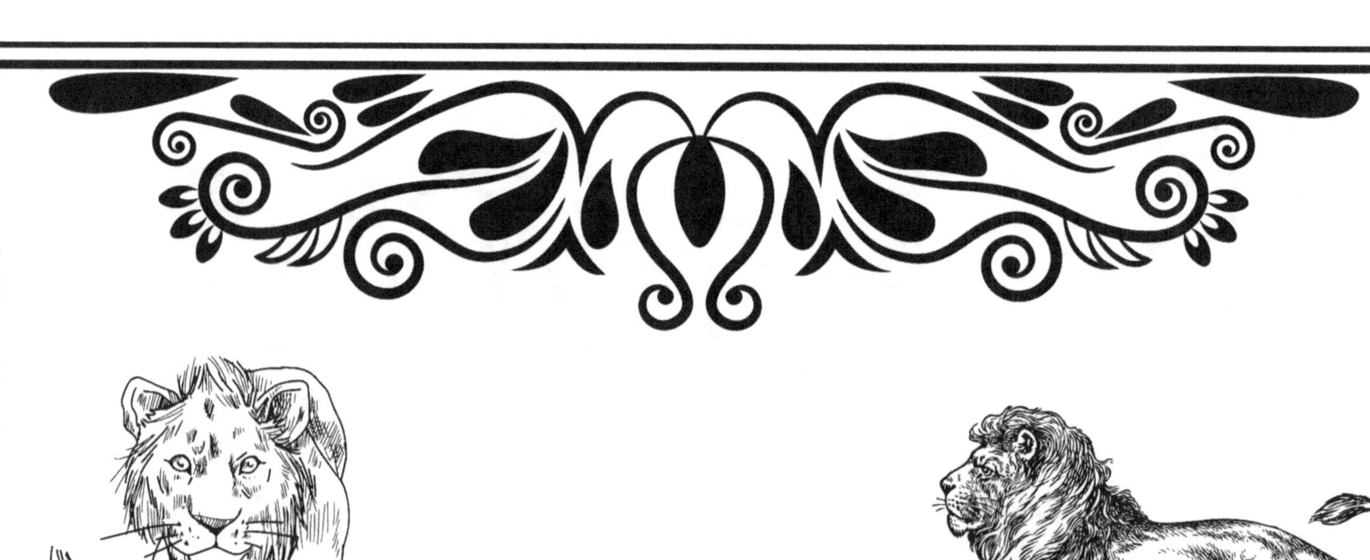

I.H.P

italo Henrique Publications

TEST COLOR PAGE

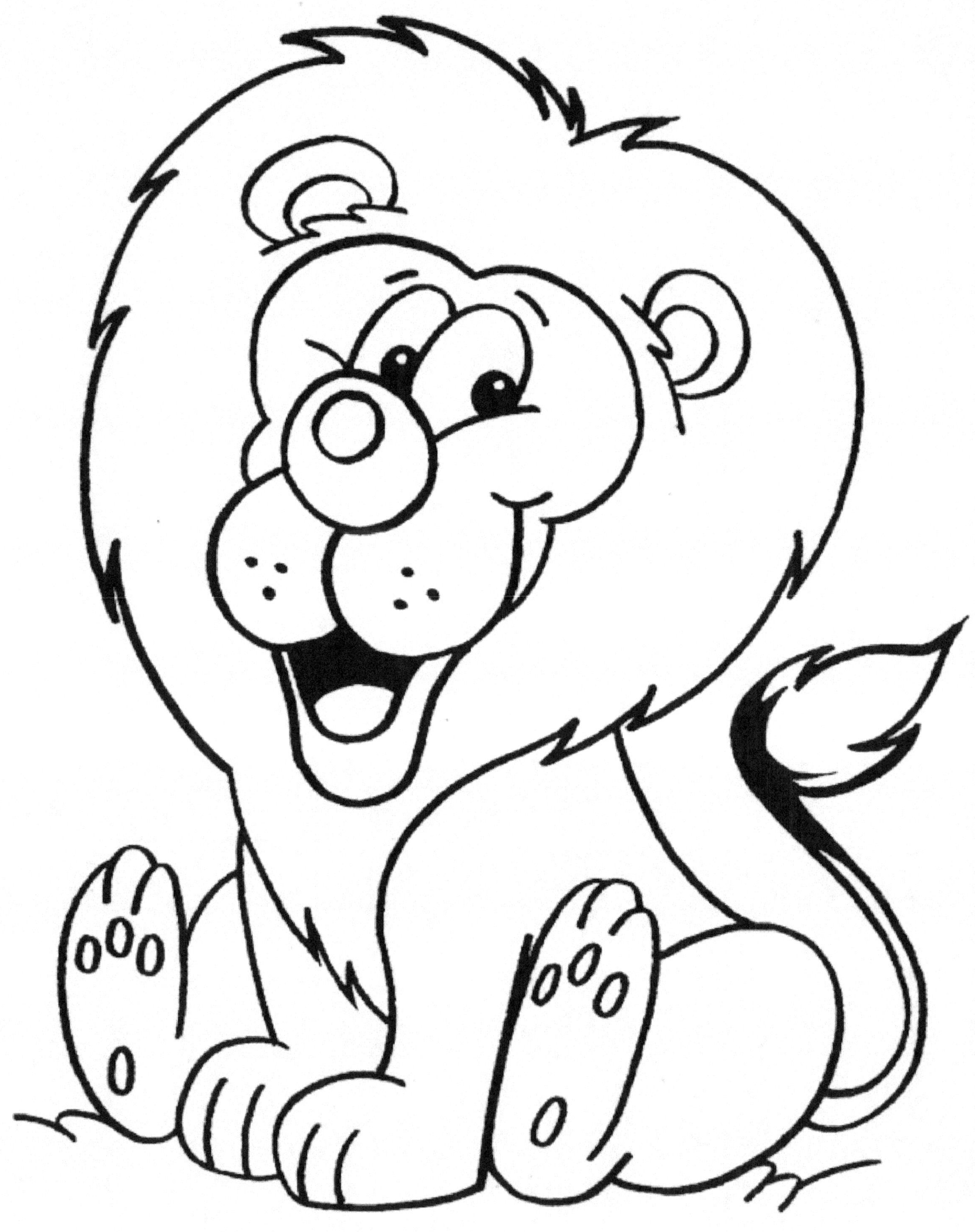

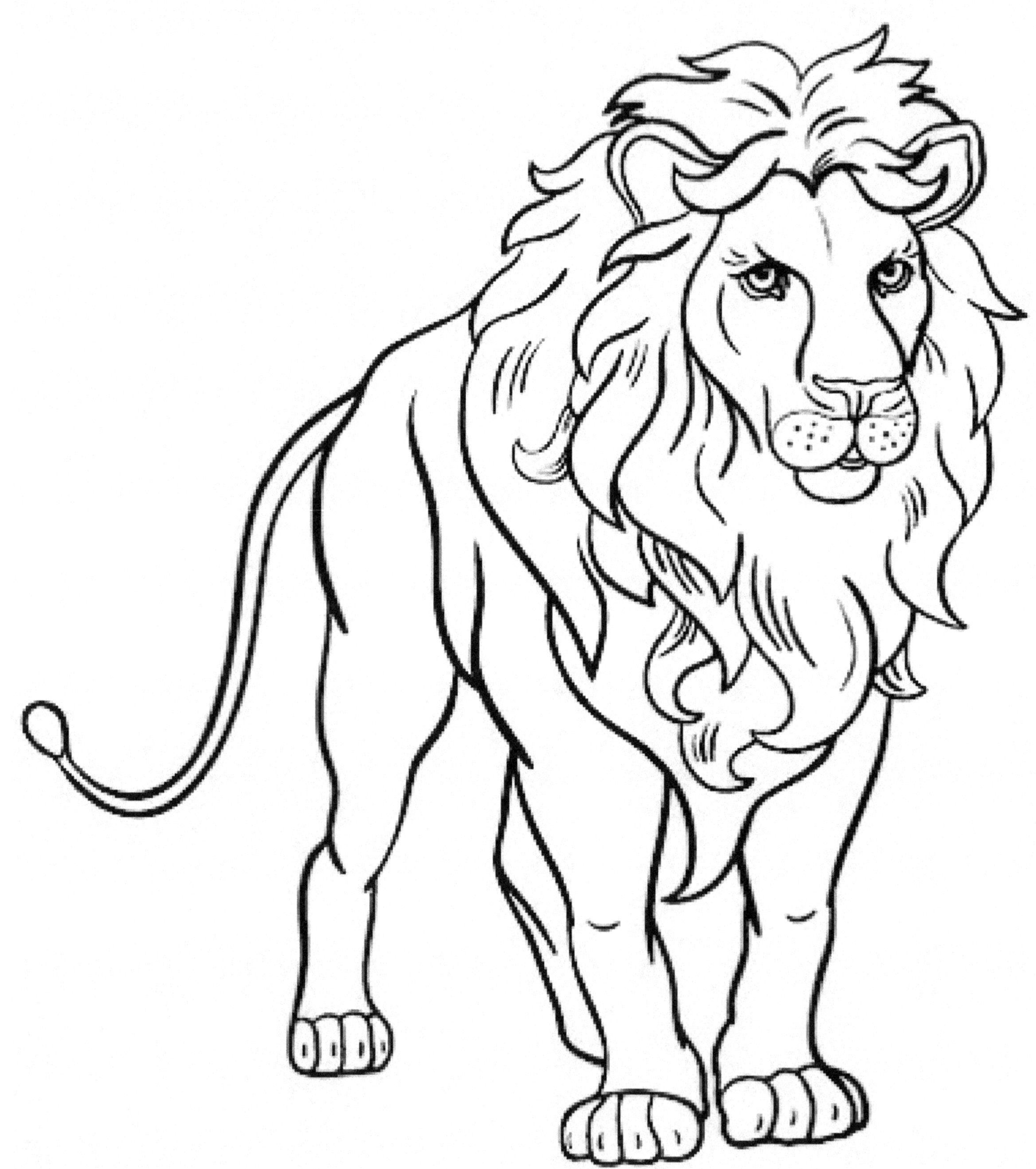

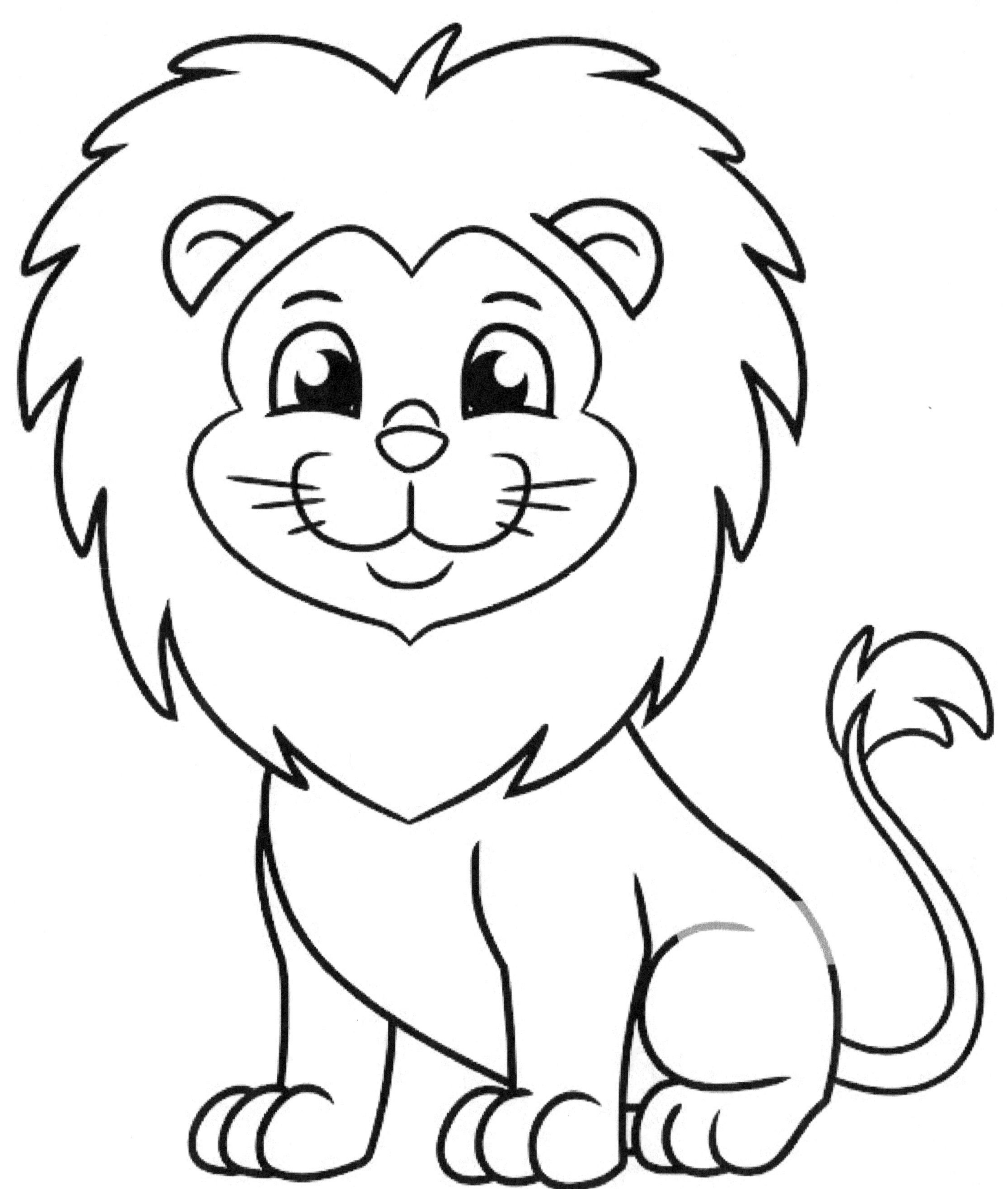

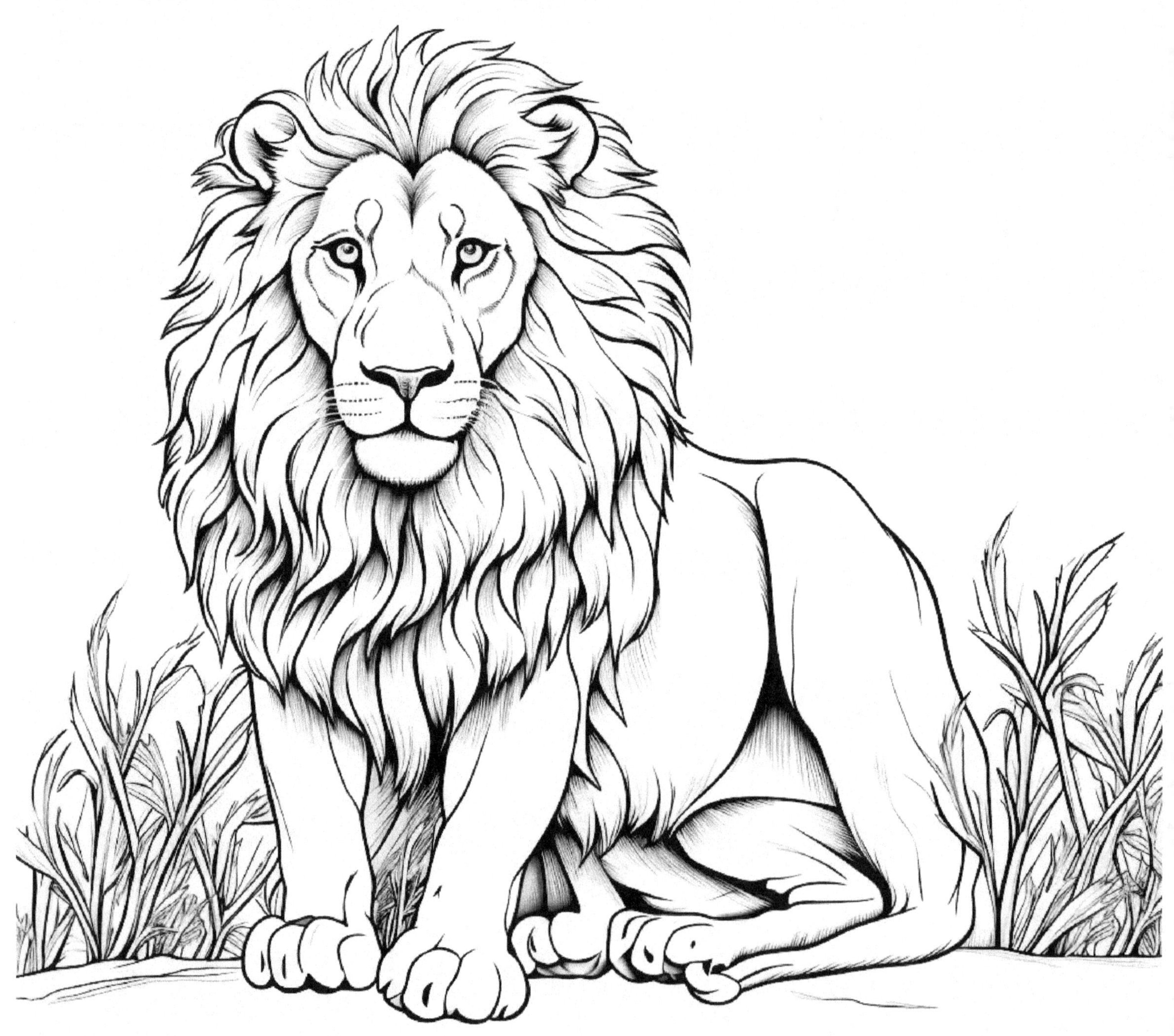

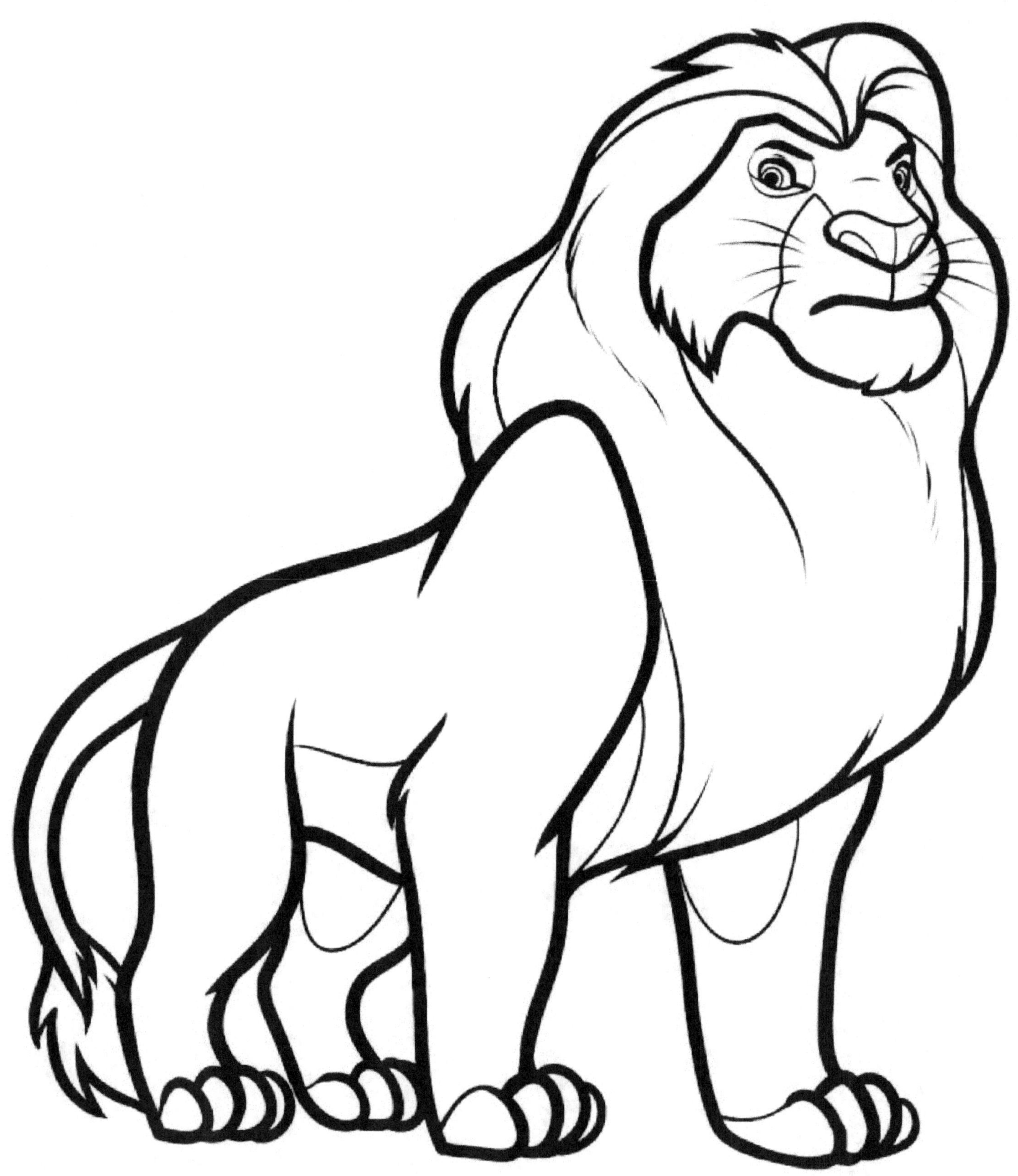

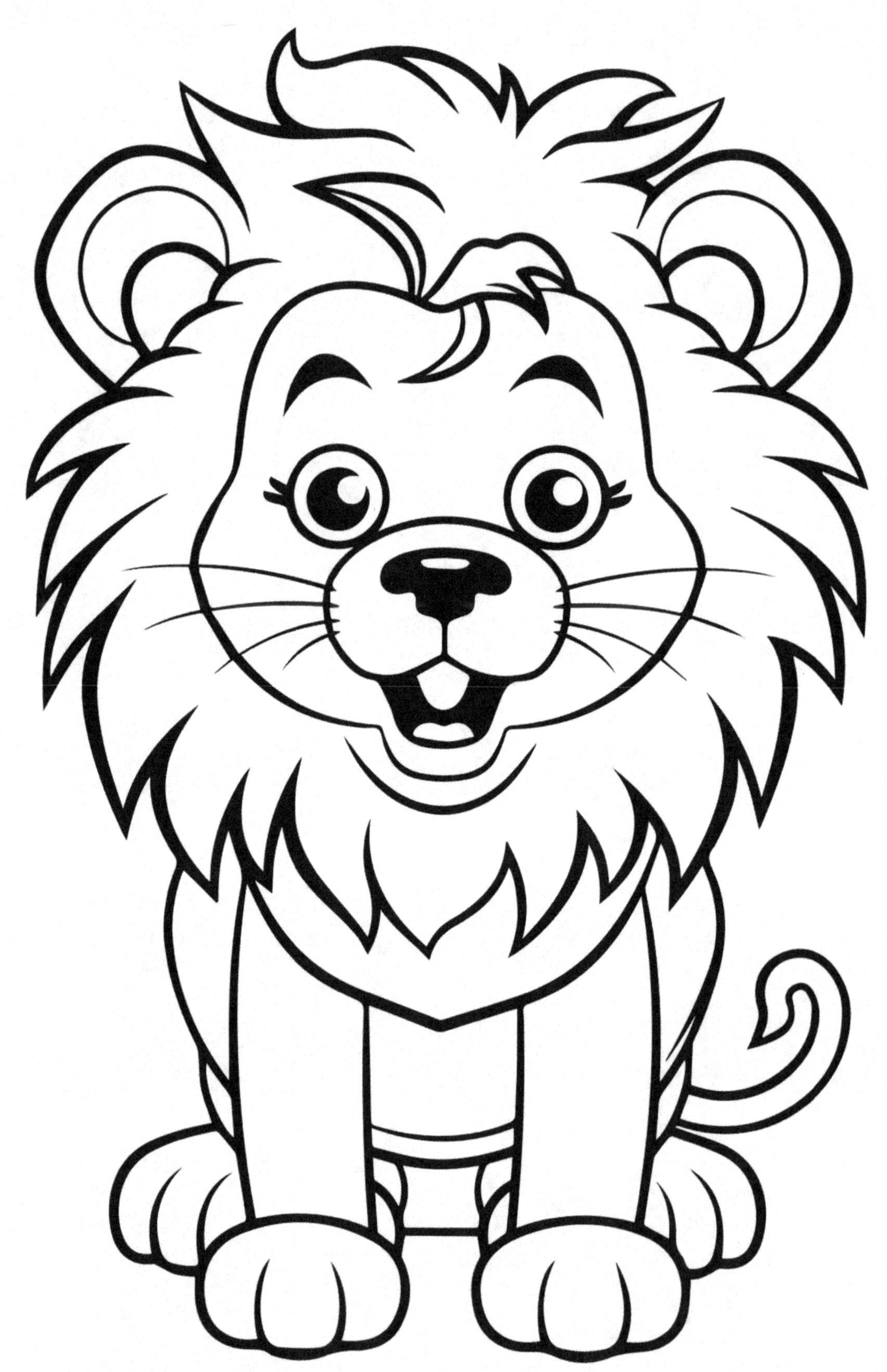

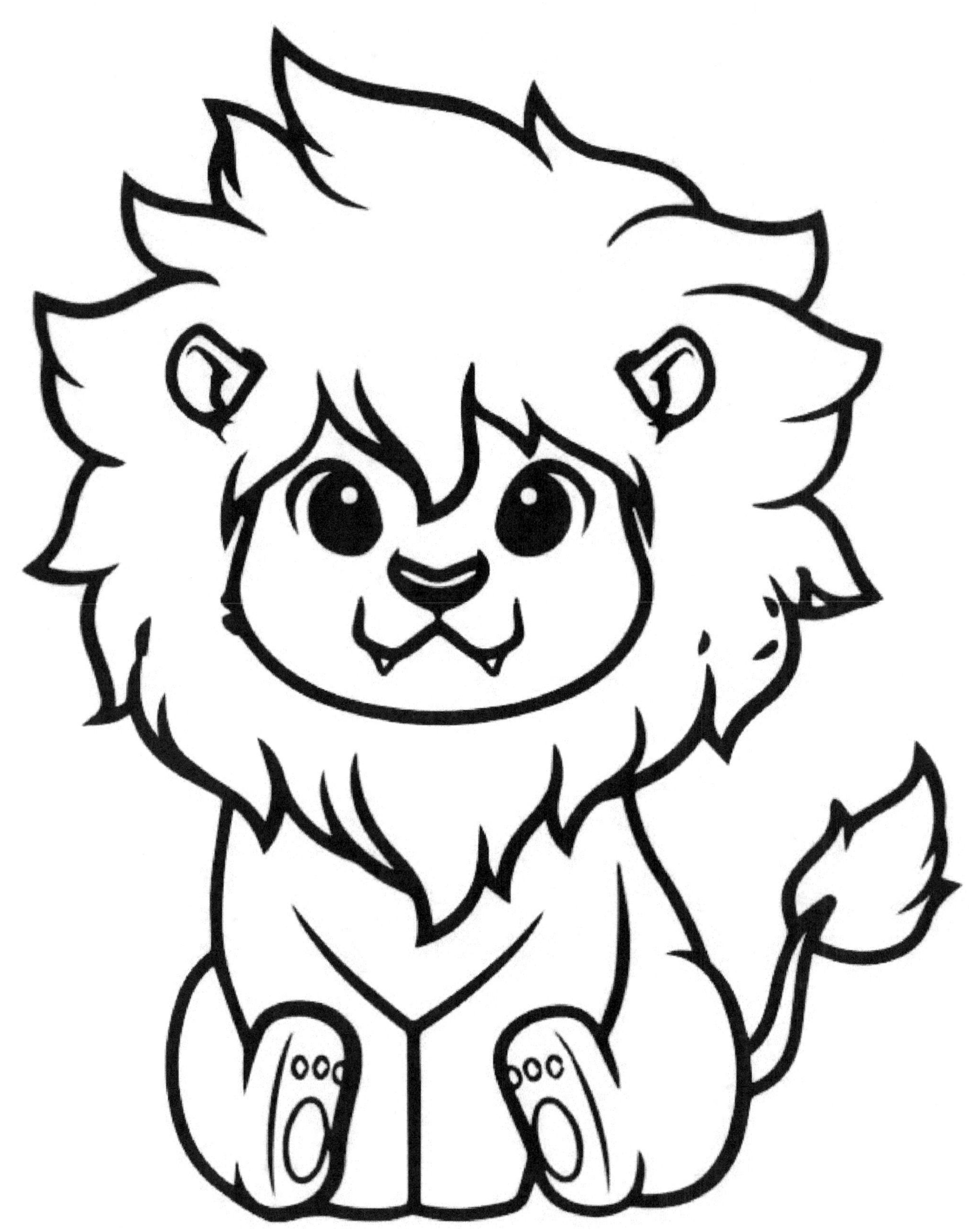

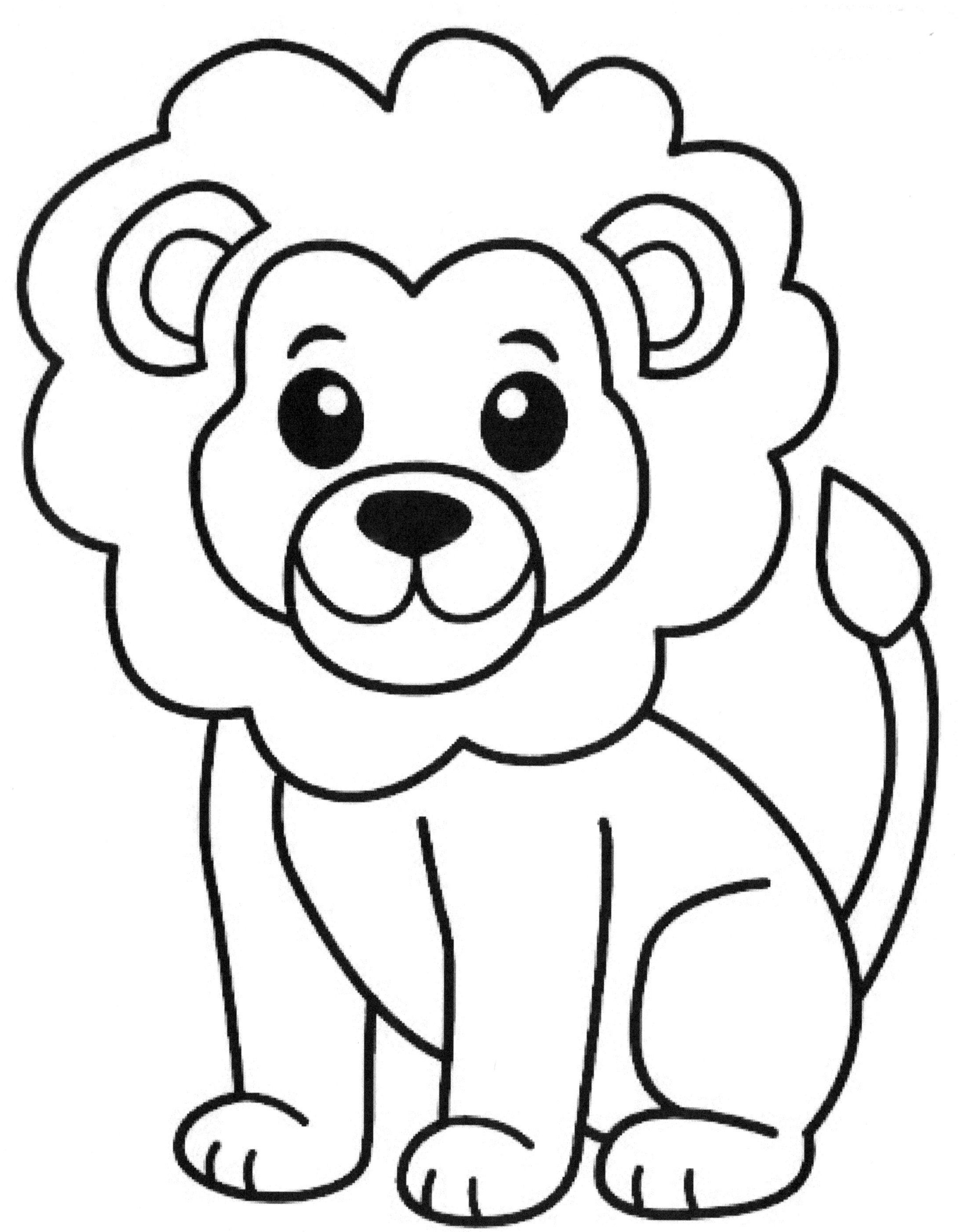

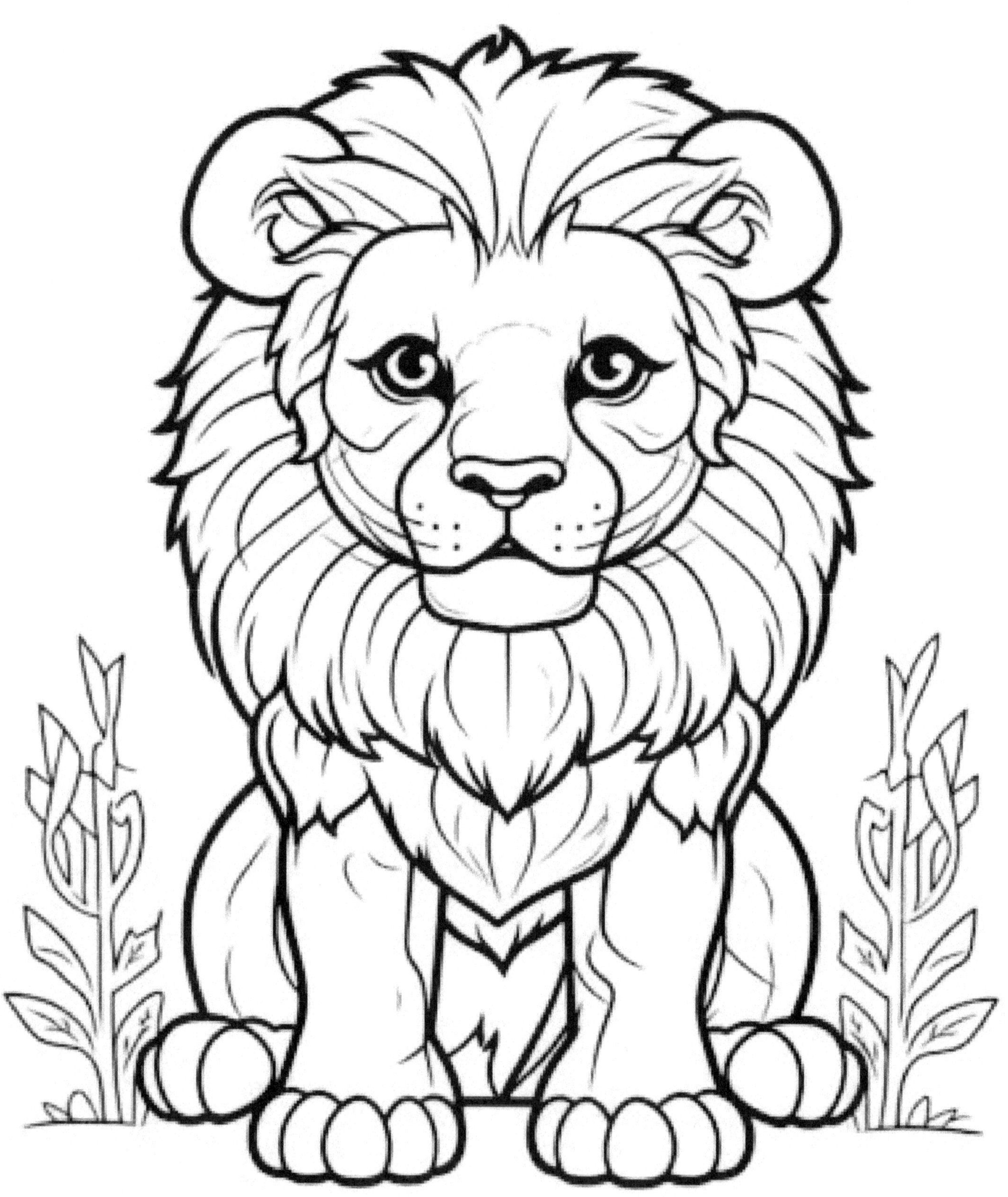

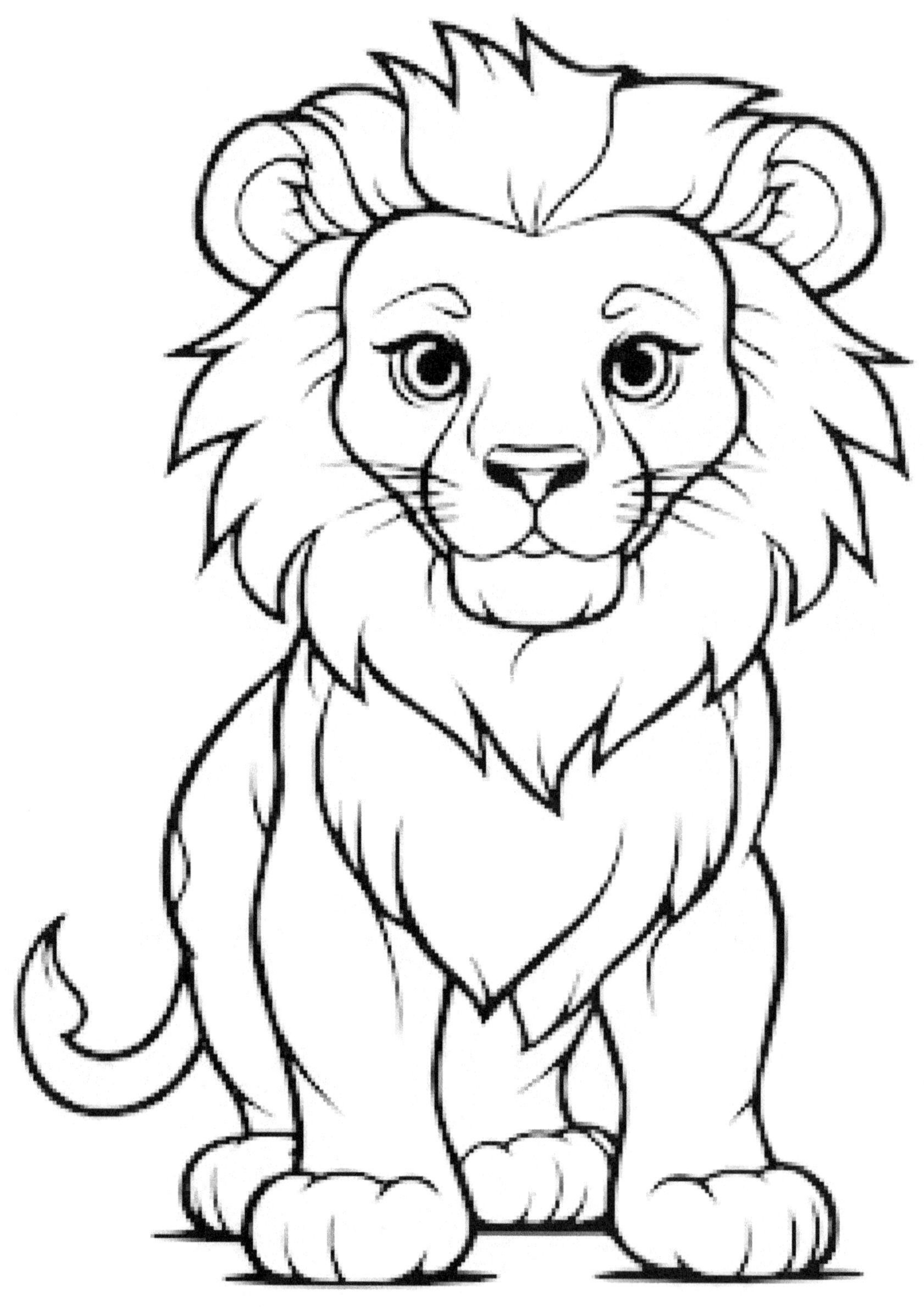

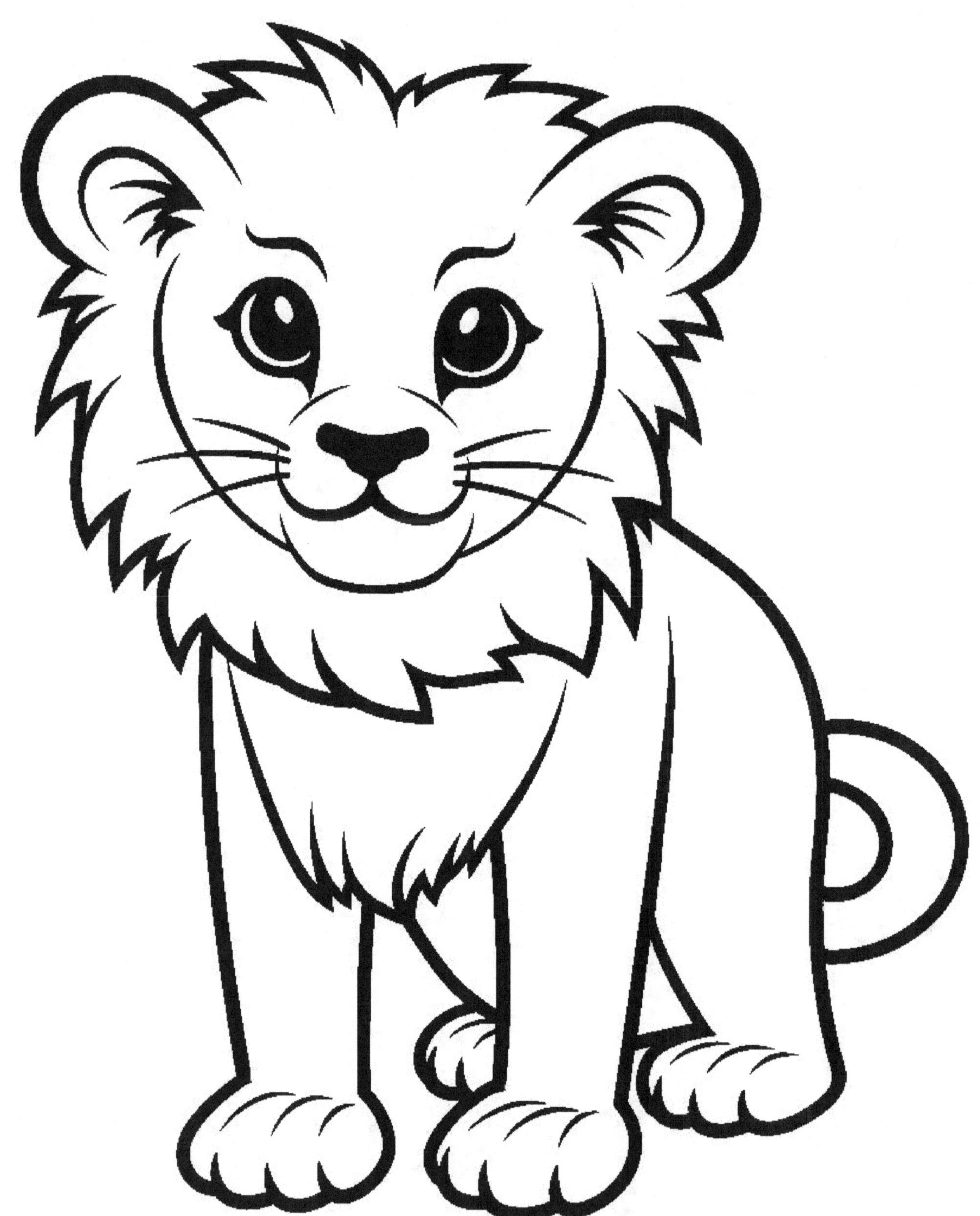

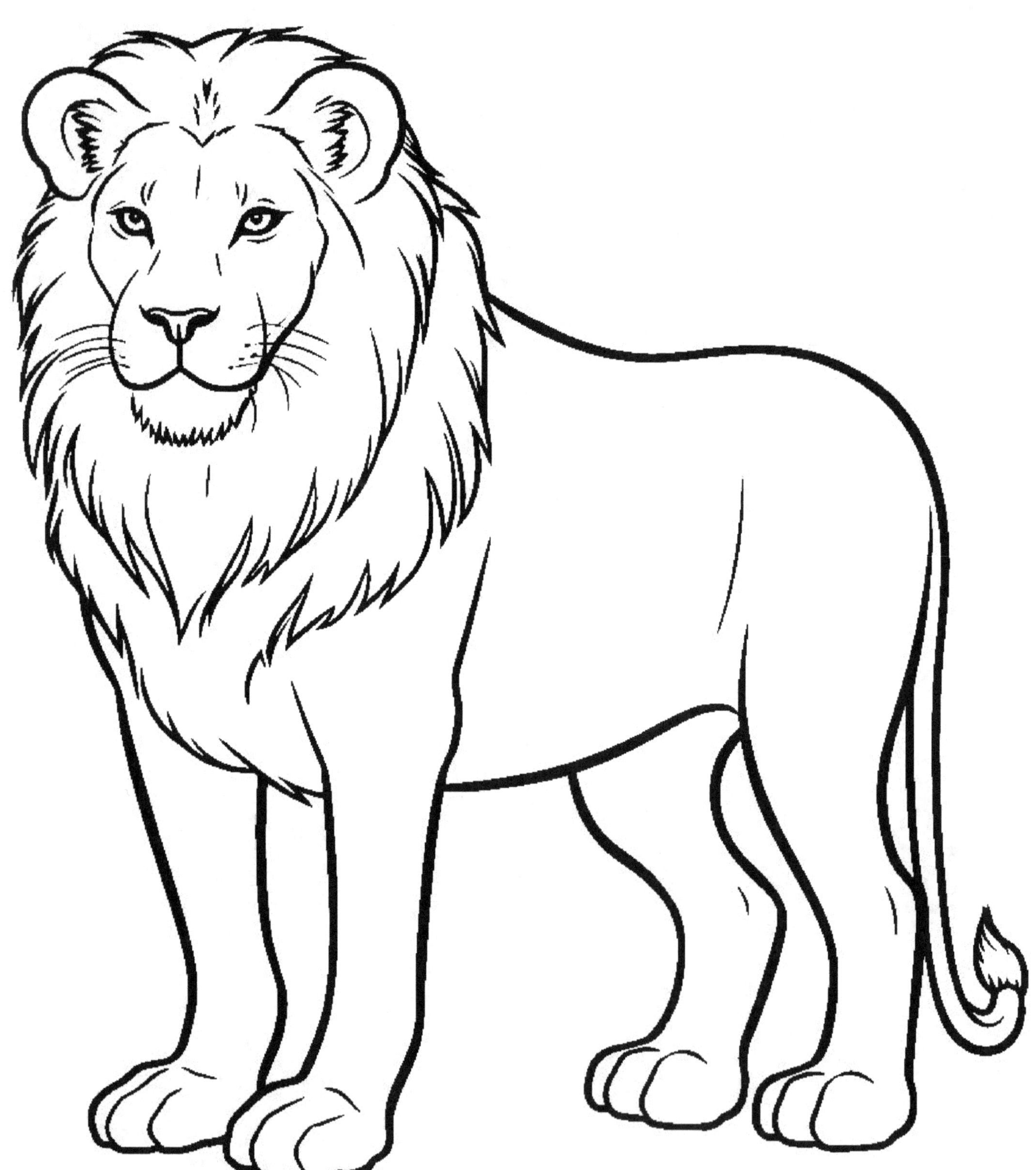

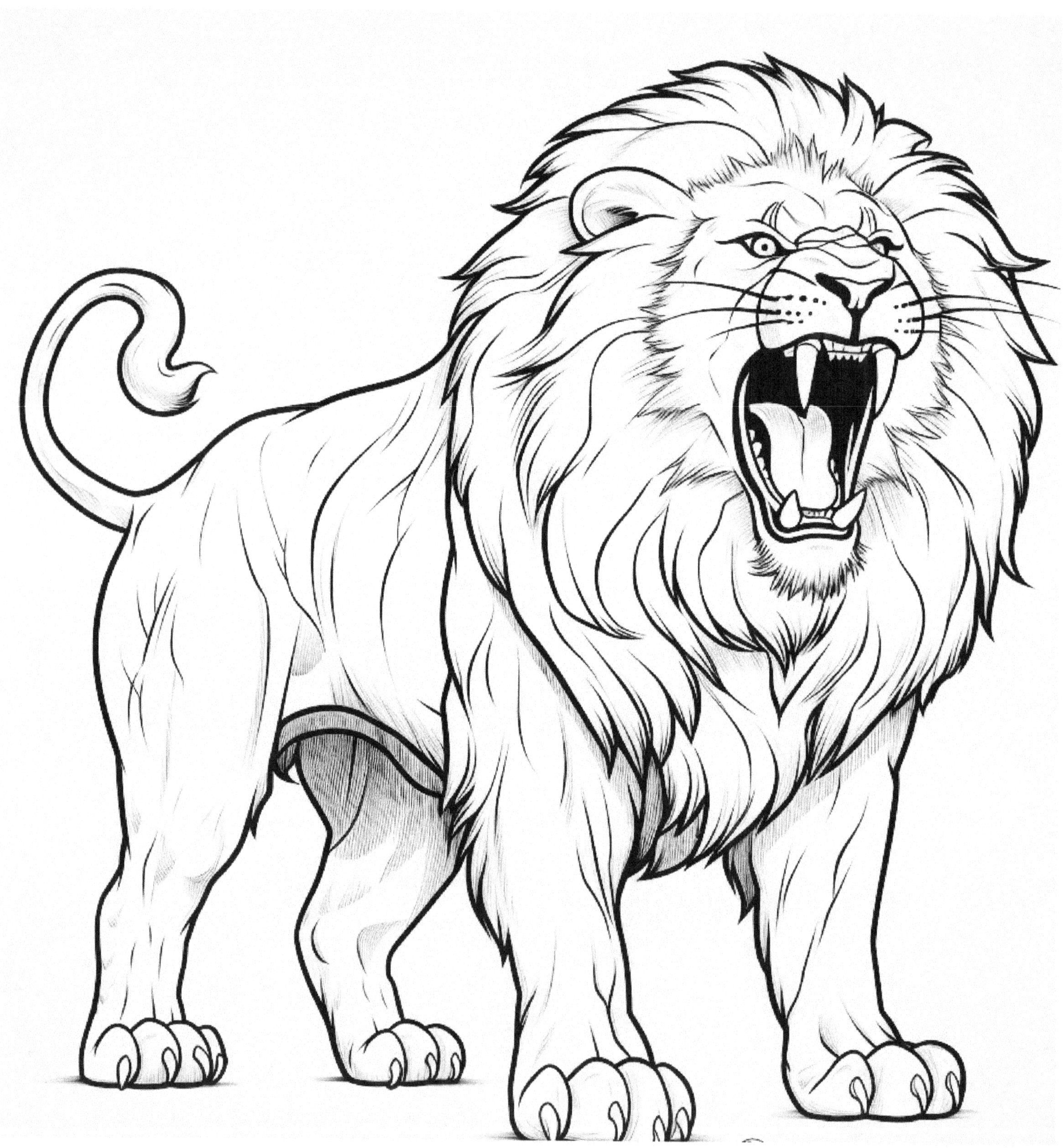

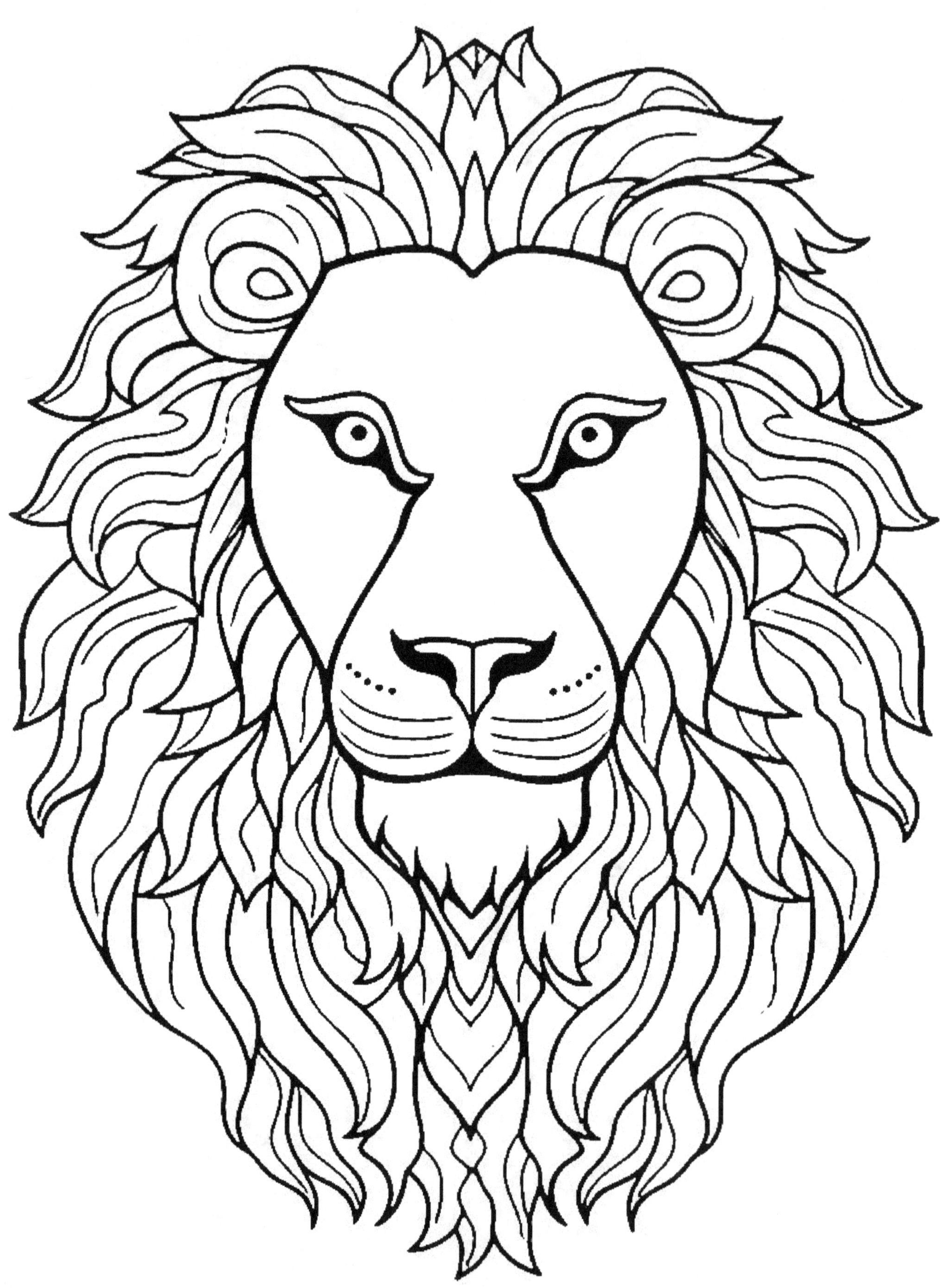

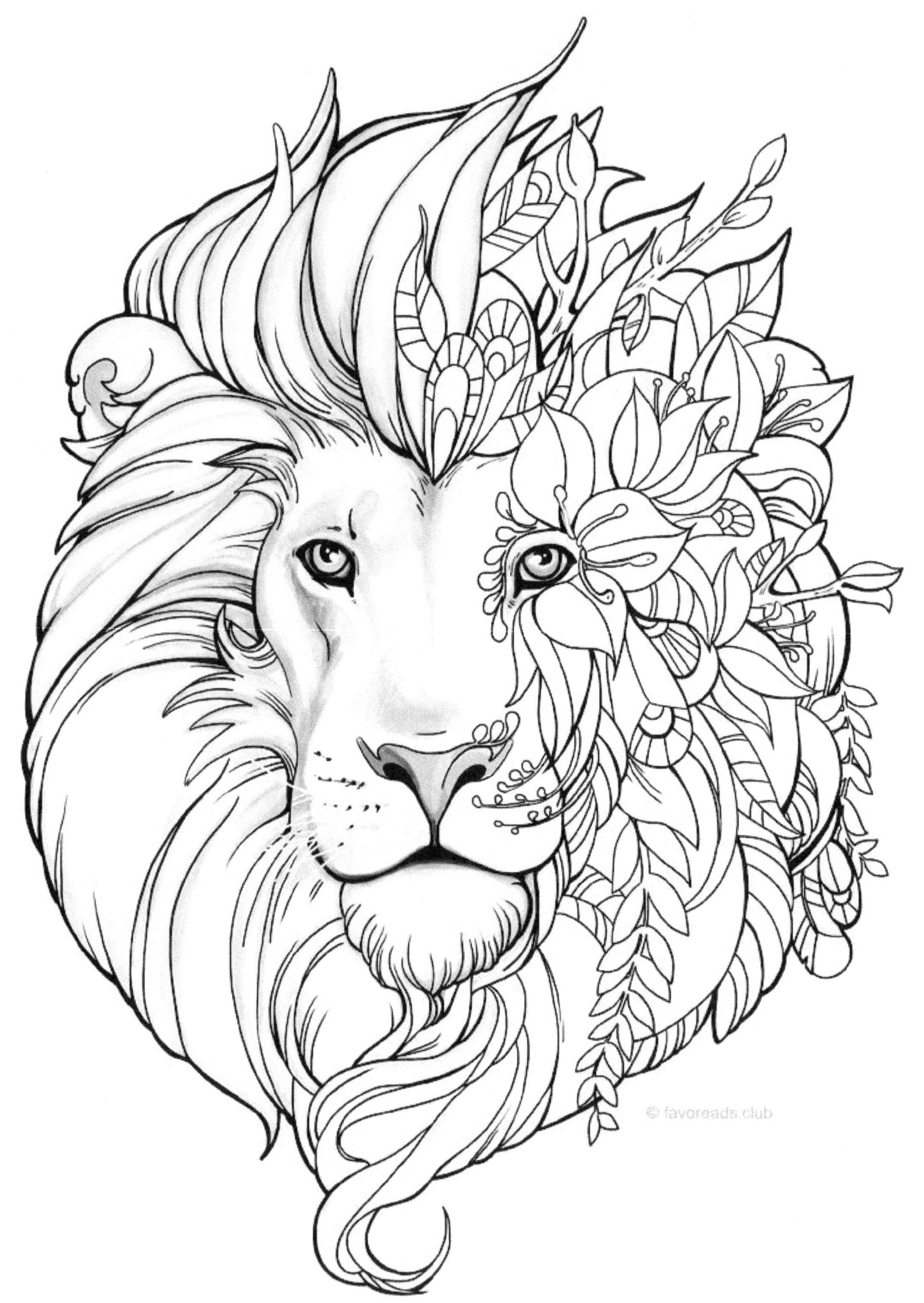
© favoreads.club

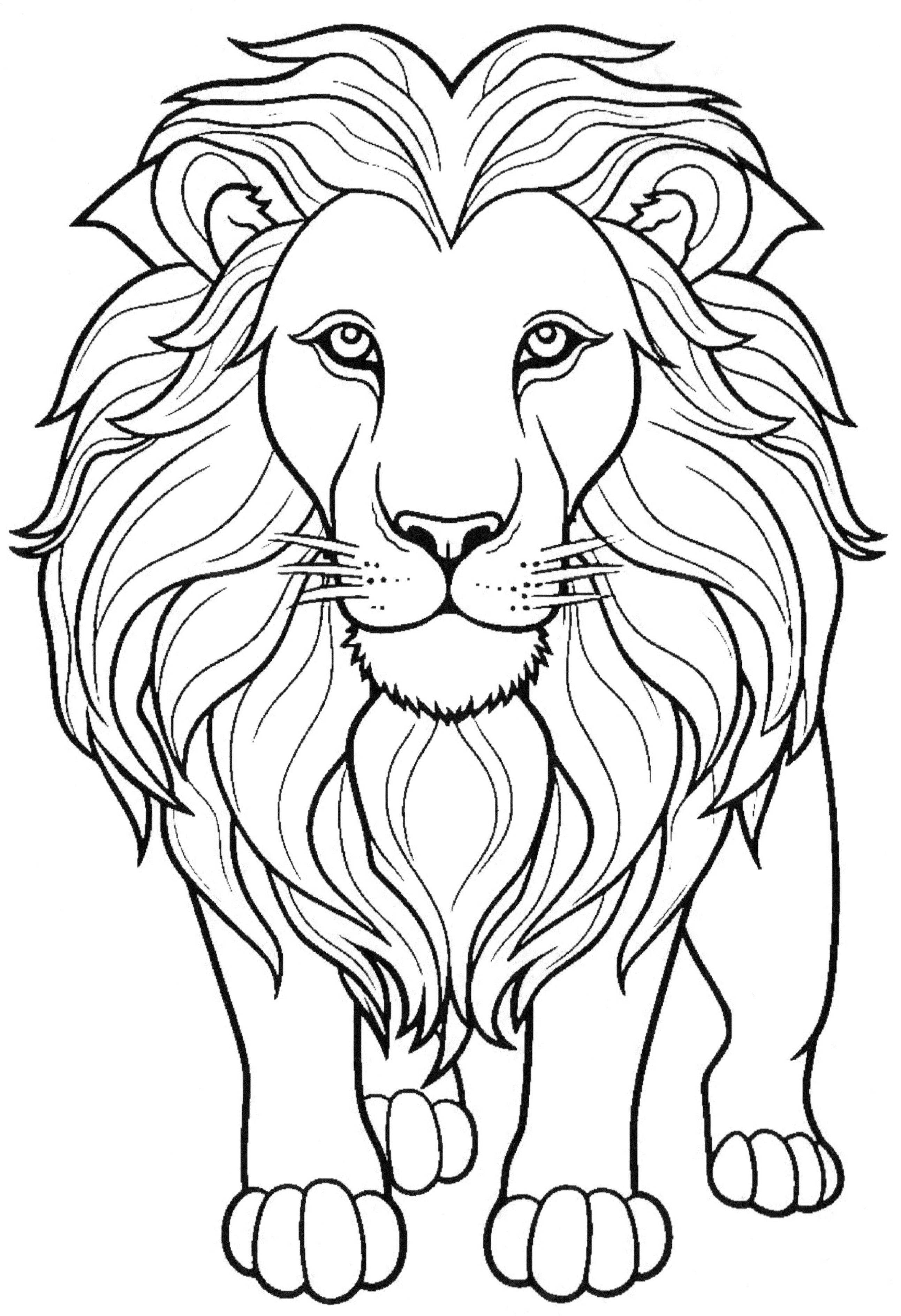

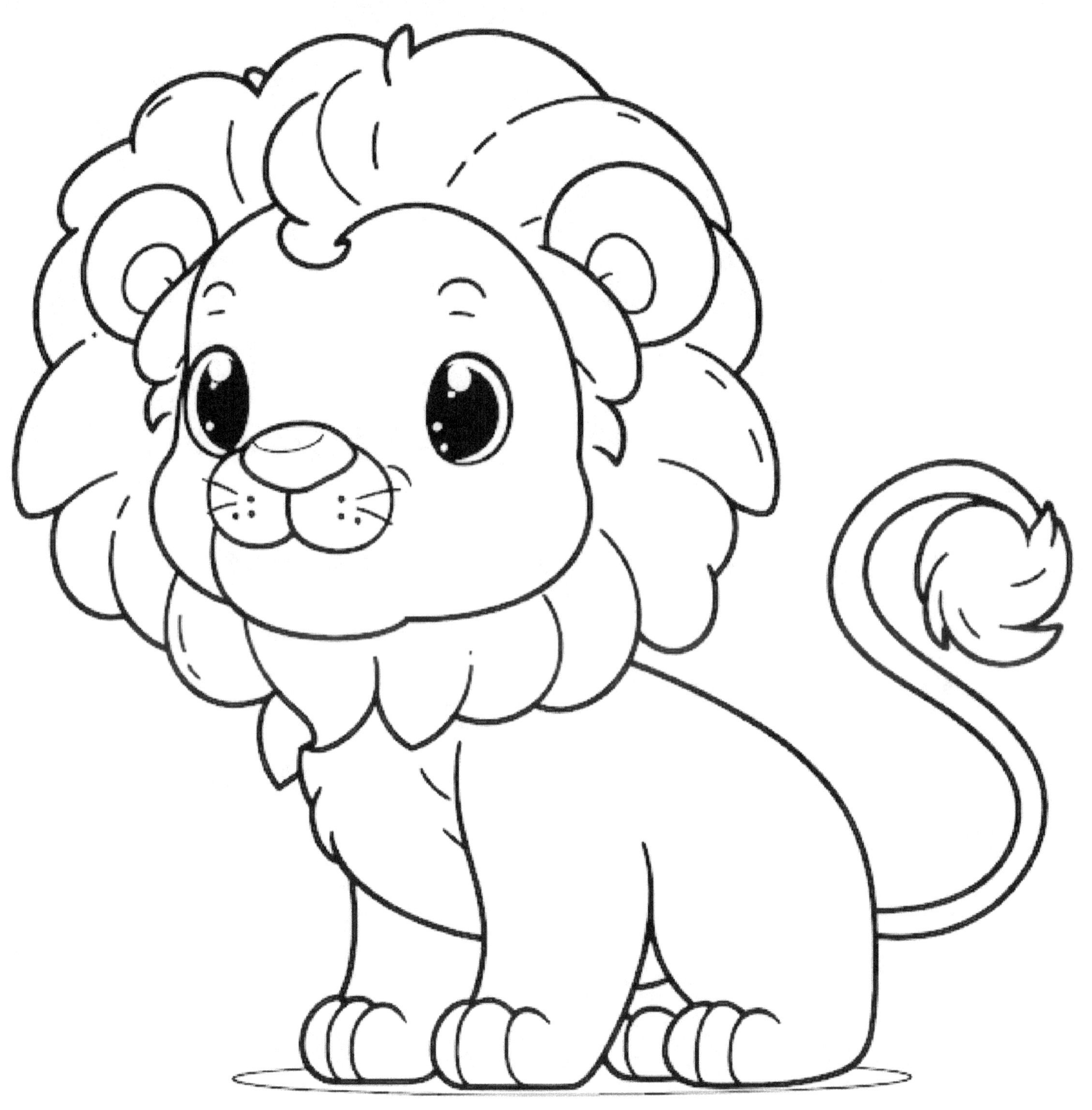